a beautiful rebellion

a beautiful rebellion

rita bouvier

Thistledown
Press

Thistledown Press Ltd.
Unit 222, 220 20th Street W
Saskatoon SK S7M 0W9
www.thistledownpress.com

Library and Archives Canada Cataloguing in Publication
Title: A beautiful rebellion : poems / Rita Bouvier.
Names: Bouvier, Rita, author.
Description: Text in English; includes some text in Michif.
Identifiers: Canadiana 20220481008 | ISBN 9781771872348 (softcover)
Classification: LCC PS8553.O8893 B43 2023 | DDC C811/.54—dc23

Epigraph from Linda Hogan in *The Radiant Lives of Animals*, Beacon Press, 2020. Used with permission.

Cover image by Mark Duffy / Alamy Stock Photo
Cover and book design by Tania Craan
Printed and bound in Canada

Thistledown Press gratefully acknowledges the financial assistance of The Canada Council for the Arts, SK Arts, and the Government of Canada for its publishing program.

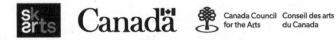

"The cure of susto, soul sickness, is not found in books. It is written in the bark of a tree, in the moonlit silence of night, along the bank of a river, and in the voice of water's motion. This cure is outside of our human selves, but it becomes the thread that connects the outer world with our own."

Linda Hogan in *The Radiant Lives of Animals*, Beacon Press, 2020.

for Matthew Joseph

Table of Contents

a beautiful rebellion

today is the first day

(*borrowed* from the title of a painting by Alex Janvier dated 1974)

hark!   the winged ones   are at it again
they are singing   so thrilled to be alive
this   surely   is goodness

look!   the sun appears on the horizon
its life force   climbing your doorstep
this   surely   is goodness

hâw!   nîsta mîna niwan'skan
iyko î miyohtamân anohckîsikâw
âw!   êkoma imiyowasik!

in gratitude   I too   will arise
so joyful for a new day
oh!   this surely is goodness!

in retrospect

(for two *aunties*, language consultation, NWT Canada, 2009)

sometimes it's hard to hide
weariness of body   exasperation of heart
even while giving expressions of love
gratitude for a language   only a few speak

having to repeat the same things
over and over   again and again
hardships facing families and community
a consequence of colonial violence

a growing resentment to consultations
talk that leads to nowhere
yet knowing the importance of
giving voice to what matters to ay'sînowak—human beings
a gift of renewal

understanding that language is the sinew
connecting us to a life force   living on the land
an intimate   endless deep listening
storied   spoken   performed   sung and danced
children learn all the language they need early
in the arms of family and a circle of community

today I was captivated by two *aunties*
walking away from our talk
one behind the other   wind delicately ruffling
their silvery grey hair and sweaters of sky and magenta

stopping on a narrow dirt path home
lingering in kinship and friendship
visiting in the language of this place
audible from where I stood

carrying ancestral memories of the land
their hopes and dreams   to future generations
mixed with laughter and kindly gestures
for one another   teaching me

what it means to live as Gwich'in!

a beautiful rebellion

women across the land
are dancing
the mighty nahannie
dehcho—the Mackenzie
misinipî—the Churchill
kâ kisiskâcowa—the Saskatchewan

the dance   the music
it goes like this
miyo-sâkihitôwin—
a sacred love for all
a round dance revolution
all can join

don your moccasins   nosisim   grandchild
join in the nîmihitowin movement   dancing
restoring the art of gathering
sweet   wild berries
mint and ginger root
restoring the art of harvesting
making dried fish
scraping and tanning moose hides
restoring the art of visiting
recounting the memories
adding to the story
like old times around the fire
giving thanks   always give thanks

iyakôma   the wise people said   this is it
î miyösik   ôma   this is goodness
kâwiya wihkâc wanikiskisik   don't ever forget this

like children

(for my friend, the late Greg Younging)

if we must take a stand   let's hold hands
skipping in time to the beat of our hearts
like we did as children long ago

when we tire   let's all fall down
in one big heap   preferably
on a bed of mustard-yellow dandelions

our eyes to the heavens   let's linger   play a while
weaving   golden sunlit dandelion crowns
bursts of radiating love for one another

later   along a rainbow of houses
let's fill the streets with verse

    So much within us.
    So much between us.
    So far apart.
    So hard to know.
    So hard.

    But a friend called madness
    gives me power to survive.

    Evading anger's blackened burden,
    I will crush decaying statues
    and [sing] out the power
    from old bones, buried

    in the land.

on every yard and boulevard   let's plant
scent and colour   gardens of edibles
so   no one goes hungry

let's promise   we will be *idle no more*
dancing as ceremony   the cosmic round dance
of a living evolutionary revolutionary universe

holy, holy, holy

(for all who work so hard to remind us that "water is life")

nipî   surrounds our island home
in my grandfather's hands
it turns into steam
bending the planking for the hull
of the coveted ribbed   canvas-wrapped canoe

it is dew at dawn
droplets of condensed water vapor
on blades of grass   on a spider's web
jewel-like
clinging their way back to the earth

it is waves crashing against the rocky shoreline
the hand of *the great mystery* for some   God
reaching in   and then out again
power to offer life
or death

it is dark   blueberry clouds
full   ripe and ready to burst
sweeping the residue of humus
into the surrounding ponds and lake
abundance in a never-ending cycle of life

on an early autumn day
setting out to check on the nets
it is mist rising off the lake
slowly turning into clouds
to bring rain another day

kapipohk   it is icicles forming   in winter
hanging on branches of trees
when ice and snow
conspire
with the sun

it is the sweet water
of birch in spring
in a cauldron over a hot fire
turning into syrupy magic
before your very eyes

it is a rupturing   a rite of passage
as baptismal ceremony   a cry
when we are born
into this place   this land
this one life

ode to the jack pine

o gangly   lean and frugal one
they say   you are our greatest defense
against climate change
our atmosphere overloaded
from our excesses   you swallow
oxygenate   make whole again

they say   you are the song
a silent infrasound
the drum
the secret of our existence
ancient   you have more DNA
than a human   you are
a powerhouse of nature

they say   you are medicinal aerosol
a rich biochemical   molecular picnic
a tree is not just a tree
you are a life-giving green machine
as a friend might   lichen love you
I am in awe of you

welcoming bear

(for Sue Goyette)

in hushed soft sounds of a language born to this land   I welcome bear out
of his slumber and cave into the spring air

hâw   tân'si   kiwan'skân cå nît'sân?   tâpwî nidîhihk ohci î miyohtamân
kâwî î wâpim'tân   piyahtak mâka   kâwiya sîk'si mîna   miyokîsikâw
miyowâsîskwan   êkwa piyîsîsak mîna nakamowak   êkohk î
miyohtahkwâw
kâwî î wâpim'skwâw   nîsta nimiyohtîn î wan'skâyin
sîkwan êkwa   êkwa ôma î miyösik   piyahtak mâka   piyahtak

hâw   greetings   are you awake now my relative?   my heart is filled with
gladness
to see you again   carefully now   don't be afraid   it is a beautiful day
the sun is shining   and birds too are singing   they are so happy
to see you again   I too am happy that you have awakened
it is spring now   this is a wondrous thing   carefully now   carefully

deeper than bone

when they ask you
who are your people?
say . . .

they are the people
who live
     in the clearing where the rivers empty
     in the narrows of beaver river valley
     in *haida gwaii*
     at the foot of the three sisters

they are the people
who live
     along the bay of *winipakw*
     along the river where bow reeds grow
     along the valley of the *l'krrâň rriviyårr*
     on top of small mountain

they are the people
who live
     where two rivers come together
     where the people fish
     where the humpback salmon spawn
     near the lizard's domain

they are the people
who live
     by the waterfall place
     by the holy springs
     by the strait of the spirit
     in the place of peace

here on turtle's back
on the land of the long white cloud
home, down under in an endless time of dreaming
the coming together   the falling apart
as it is today and forever

the mirroring of the soul was always there in front of us

in the new greening of spring
bursting on the tips of branches
when we awoke one morning

in the larger than night-sun sinking
into the far   dark blue horizon
as we meandered home   weary

in long shadows of poplar trees
in the sweet scent of leaves
crackling beneath our feet

in the crystals of ice forming
glistening as the sun refracted
its rays straight into our soul

a place I know

soundscape

the secret of all things gone   the whispering
of every leaf   the rushing
of the river downstream   the swishing
of cattails in the wind   the whooshing
of eagle wings on the rise   the nibbling
of mice underground   the grunting
of foraging bears deep in the forest
the saddest sound you will ever hear
is the faint and mournful sound
of a beaver crying

    tapwe!   this is the truth

he had lost everything he had
his mate   all his offspring
their habitat destroyed by human hands
making way for more
and more

a place I know

at the mouth of the Canoe River
yôtin is arrested   stillness   wind

sound amplified   nature's symphony playing
a harmony of wings   quacks and splashes

as each sound seeps into my weary body
a memory comes rushing in   harvesting duck eggs

the warmth of the sun on my back
moshôm motioning directions   *nitânis ôtî*   my daughter over here

he says   as we weave quietly   ceremoniously
through tall reeds   ducks scattering

today   sîpî is a mirrored sky of blue and white   the river
I dip my paddle into   ever so delicately

keeping time   as I churn wispy clouds sailing by below me
look!   I whisper to my canoeing companion

pointing to the lily pads   pops of yellow surprise
as perfect backdrop on this glorious day

the waterway lined with obedient   bowing reed heads
is the path   taking us into the interior!

he hasn't entirely lost his touch

patched canvas carpenter's apron on
he inspects the basic tools of his trade
making sure everything is in working order
the old hammer has not lost its head
an inclination to do so of late
the screwdriver isn't missing parts
its shank or blades
the wood chisel is as sharp as it can be
with power to scrape and shape
the old   tattered cloth measuring tape
and bite-sized   chewed-up pencil
are within reach for accuracy and precision
a tendency to stray these days
the small framing square and miniature level
are where they need to be
with everything else   for balance

then   there are odds and ends
nails and screws   washers and nuts of all sizes
recycled wires of various thicknesses
left-over leather strapping
and oh yes   discarded string
awâsisak kici   for the children
at home with their mothers

he grabs the small whetstone
off the shelf where he left it last night
after sharpening knives someone dropped off
he remembers the large whetstone by the old shed
a hobby and practice of sharpening axes and saws
for villagers when the work was done

finally   he checks for his pocketknife
he carries with him all the time
handy for scraping off the corrosion
of the forgotten   rust and time

he hasn't entirely lost his touch
but   he can no longer perform
the heavy lifting of dragging
wet   tangled-with-weed nets
out of the lake into the skiff
he can no longer journey out
into the forest alone for the day
to hunt game
his sight failing

now   he is content simply to be of use
to his daughters-in-law
or to someone in the village today
and the next day if need be
all for the art of
a visit and a cup of tea

a winter's day in Île Bouleaux

some say   *you can never go back*
maybe that's true   I think to myself
heading out across the lake on snowshoes
light snow falling
as I navigate drift piles
to my childhood island home

once on land   I notice tracks
dogs   wolves more likely
always plenty here
where fisherman often leave behind
offerings to the wild

the place where the old log cabin stood
is a ruin
an overgrowth of brush   the fallen
birch and poplar trees
their frost covered   naked branches
shimmering sunlight   beauty
at its height

there are few signs of human habitation
except for the odd notched log here and there
I stop to search for my favourite lookout
where I waited for the pinpoint of my papa
to return from a day's work   across the frozen lake

my sight set on the shoreline
I tramp carefully
toward what was once a launch site
for boats in summer
horse-drawn sleds in winter
when my snowshoe catches
a hidden   fallen tree
bringing me to the ground
on my knees

there I am   face to face
with an iron-rubber strapping
anchored to the side of a tree stump
a place to tie
to rest weary horses
while papa stopped
for a cup of afternoon tea
in an instant   I am home
overcome   I sit in the snow
bound in an emotional tangle
trying to recover from the fall

I recall   like it was yesterday
how dutifully I would fetch water
from the lake for the horses
watch them sip quietly
as the heat from their bodies
rose   steaming the air around them
in a wonderland   on a winter's day

nîso lî batô

two boats sit in the dusk
in faded colours of blood red and sky blue
rising and falling on the rippling
of waves beneath their hulls

each is tethered to a rickety plank-board
dock   flanked by towering reeds
that will overtake the shoreline
once they are gone

in companionship   they sit patiently
waiting for their owners to show
greasy gasoline outboard motors
hand-carved   cherished paddles in hand

for now   they are content
just to rest side by side
like two old friends
comfortable with silence

who goes to their death willingly?
who doesn't want to take
    just one more ride
down the river and back?

at the skating rink with my cousins

(for my cousins — Sister Josie, George, Linda, vye, cipep, cijô)

in anticipation of our flight tonight
we arrive at the dimly lit skating rink
its dome-shaped fixtures catching light
against a dark blue and endless sky
a perfect backdrop for a night of illusion
as gigantic snowflakes   whirl down
to earth from the heavens above

lying on our backs   in a straight line
gazing skyward   arms outstretched
snow angels on a blue-lit winter night
we prepare ourselves for the launch
and wait and wait
for the magic
of staring into a mass of feathery snowflakes
whirling down from the heavens above
to finally take effect

suddenly   all together   we are airborne
soaring higher and higher
until   we are weightless
masses of pure joy   laughter
carrying us   into the stratosphere

mama son toh-tôm

(for my late sister, Flora)

if you were here   I would remind you
call to you in a language that spells our relationship
me in relationship to you—nisîmis

if tomorrow could just be another day
I would promise to laugh at every silly joke you crack
an act of speaking the truth—tâpwêwin

I would wipe away every tear you cry
then   I would hold you tightly and never let you go
a sacred act of love—miyo sâkihitowin

I would call on all our loved ones gone before us
to lift the heavy sadness in your heart
an act of giving strength—sohkihtamân'win

just so you could stay a little longer
to lift our spirits with your gift of laughter
an act of joyfulness—môcikihtâwin

dark skies over South Bay

in the late lazy hot afternoon buzz
grandfather yôtin prepares a storm

whooshing through
tall pine trees standing in front of n'dânis' postage-stamp house

home to her chirpy   chatty but neighbourly friends
with whom she shares her toast and jam

she watches them scurry
up and down the old missionary pine trees

back and forth across the fence line
in excitement   their exuberant tails can't hide

nearby the jacketed bumblebees are a-buzz
hovering over clover at home in her yard

in the distance   lî tanårr
begin their slow low rumbling sound

more insistent than before   yôtin
picks up speed in gusts and swirls

catches the windchime on the eaves
enchants graveyard spirits nearby

pushes her hard against her back
urges her   *run for cover*

still   she sits   caught in a daydream
of what changes   what stays the same

remembers two women at the beach earlier
sitting on a blanket   their legs outstretched

their unrestrained laughter on this hot summer day
as clouds swelled and sky grew dark

crows and ravens call out in chorus
a storm is coming   a storm is coming!

beachside   lî cilowî too call   *sandpipers*
a storm is coming   a storm is coming!

. . . and then lightning cracks
its whip across the southern sky over the graveyard

too close for comfort   sky releases
a torrential soaking downpour   as she runs

inside   drenched and dripping   covering
lî lal'mwårr facing windows just like her grandmother taught her

strangely she never takes this action
living in the city and wonders why

listening to stone

nikiskisin—I remember
when he found me   resting on the earth
the sureness of his rough   calloused
hands picking me up   caressing my roundedness

kayas—it was long ago
the contour of my body
not as shapely as you see it here today
now stripped naked of its sinew
connecting me to the hardwood
of this forest

nikiskisin—I remember
the indescribable joy I felt
as I was lifted from the ground
rolled over and over
in my relative's warm hands

studying me in the stillness
of a boreal silence
nît'sân wanted to take me back to his village   my relative
but not before the spirit-energy
relating me to this place
had been given proper thanks

at the village   my new form
slowly took shape   as he chiseled
at my mid-section
of waxy black flint with flecks of gray
rock on rock   raw energy
temperature rising   rising
sparks flying in every direction

I am the ancient one   the wise one
the one to count on
for difficult work to be done

asinî niya—I am stone

in a valley of endless time

I enter the valley
into a canopy of green
the scent of wild
rose is intoxicating
it needs no translation
I wonder why
wild roses smell like no other
their chemistry calling
bees and humans alike

the wind stirs
leaves of saskwatôminahtik   saskatoon berry bush
wolfwillow   lulling me
I close my eyes
to a sea of sound
imagine I am standing
somewhere else   close
to a large body of water
drinking all its goodness

there is decay all around
almost odorless
so it goes
everything dies
surrenders itself to the small
.creatures and invisible life-forms
unsung heroes of recycling
on this northern prairie floor

high   high overhead
in the gray-blue expanse of sky
all is not what it seems
as magpie struggles
against a whipping wind

deeper into the valley
I spot a clearing
a place to stand   to gaze beyond
where land and sky meet
I smile to see wapiti
on a nearby bluff
statuesque
for a split second
before it returns to feeding
ears-twitching   tail-flicking

I hold my breath
behold all its beauty
too quickly wapiti bounds
out of sight
I cannot make it stay
a reminder   once again
we are last in the order of things

then comes
a rushing wall of sound
piyîsîsak are out in full force today   the small, winged ones
foraging the valley   for what's left
chirping   tweeting   whistling
as they pick their fair share

the scent of sage is enveloping
before I can even see
its low-lying   silvery-gray leaves
waving at me
just then a tiny flame-coloured bird flies past me
I cry out
hey   hey   I know you   come back!
mô petit chândel   come back!

one late autumn day

stored deep   in the cool   dark earth
I discovered
the hazelnut had lost its sting
with no regard for my sister squirrel
I stripped her nest and took it all

you should have heard the clatter
the desperate chatter and scurry
a red willow switch-stick in hand
moshôm appeared and without a word
directed my rump to a tree stump
my punishment   quiet reflection
in an open field   in the hot sun

that day   I learned an important lesson
it was too late for squirrel
to replenish her cache
it was too late for me
to reverse my actions
the damage done

in reconciliation
I write and rewrite
this pathetic poem
for forgiveness
as if it is enough   will ever be enough

supermoon rising

blood on the snow

(after an installation by Rebecca Belmore, 2020, *Facing the Monumental*)

pristine and snow-white
an oversized   fluffy quilt
covers the gallery floor
ambushing the eyes
on top
in the middle of the expanse
sits   a canonical   institutional
      chair
covered in the same material as the quilt
blood-   red paint
      dripping
from the upper reaches of its frame

there's a story   here
blood on the snow
a re-membering
of the slain   the dead
a monumental human tragedy

      sometimes she is uncertain   if the human heart
      can be transformed

on December 29   1890
the night following the massacre
at Wounded Knee
it snowed and snowed
blanketing the blood-strewn
bodies of men   women and children
slaughtered as they tried to escape
miles deep into the gulch

such *a terrible beauty*   to borrow a phrase
in the images created by the story left behind

a journalist notes
just a day before   children
played innocent games
leapfrog   bucking horse . . .
now fallen
like grass before the sickle

there is solace in knowing   there is spirit stirring
inside every one of us   life released to the cosmos upon our last breath

facing the monumental

(after Rebecca Belmore, 2020)

the massive weight of colonial history
towers
over us

memory
of the theft of land
called as discovery   laws enacted to protect thieves

the absurd science
some are more human than others
a power and privilege of the fair-skinned   only

the supremacy of males
prodigious   religious   patriarchy
an indictment of church and state
we are left to mourn   kin like Cindy Gladue   rendered dispensable

an erasure of being
children separated from their families
at Sacred Heart   *sacred heart!*   Residential School
collateral damage   lateral violence in our homes and communities

an invisible injury of the 60s scoop
an unending search for kin
babies   babies!
taken from their mothers at birth

loved ones in poverty
eastside Vancouver
Saskatchewan Federal Penitentiary
it's all the same thing

                    a dead beaver
                debris and sewage washed up
            along shorelines of lakes and rivers
            where people still hunt and gather
            left with only monumental words
        to climb
        d e c o l o n i z a t i o n
    i n d i g e n i z a t i o n
r e c o n c i l i a t i o n

the great uncertainty
where does making it right begin?
in truth telling   in healing and forgiveness
or   in justice and economic parity?
does it matter where we begin?

still
in this uncivil
unholy state we find ourselves in
we are called upon   to re-member
our deep ecological relationship to all life
to re-member   what the wise ones say
it is up to you   it is up to you
to take back your humanity and selfhood
to re-member   your body is more than male or female
two-spirit is being queer and Indigenous
an arrow in a bow that intersects the hard lines drawn
balance   most importantly
to re-member   being Indigenous is immensely human

as we climb our way   into the light
we are called to *community*   the world we inhabit in need of repair
its fissures and polarizations   monstrous extremist movements on the rise
mining miniscule differences for electoral power
and as more human beings arrive from distant shores   seeking refuge
we are reminded to be welcoming   to show remarkable human kindnesses
there are no red yellow black or white races

facing the monumental
    we look beyond ourselves to others
    human and non-human
    with whom we share this marbled blue and green planet
facing the monumental
    we imagine respectful relationships
    an ethos of protecting the life that gives us life
    we are last in the order of things
facing the monumental
    we address the betrayal of thinking in policy and legislation
    enacted by self-serving politicians   more interested in power
    than bettering our human lives and our relationships
facing the monumental
    we create nurturing spaces of love and kinship
    belongingness and empathy   laughter and joyfulness
    beauty   everywhere we stand
facing the monumental
    is necessarily extra-ordinary!

something about her

(for a friend)

I married young   to escape the violence
in my home   and society in general   she says
I lean in to listen
something about her
a quiet resolve to be her own person
a fighter for the love of her children
her family   possibly the whole human race
an academic who has studied the history
of Indigenous North American arts
a museum curator

she painstakingly recalls   her escape
from emotional and physical abuse
from the fathers of her children
to pursue her own dreams   of creation
to surround herself with beauty
to transcend the madness   ugly stereotypes
the effects of history   colonization
its impact on her   her family   her community

she recalls the fateful day she decided
it was time to take the risk
study south of the border   accepted
to a prestigious Indigenous fine arts school
to take to the road with all her children in tow

she recalled   the hardest part was listening
to her children plead with her   to return home
how frightened she was   as she crossed
the threshold   of the Wyoming border
the rise of land   obscuring the light
she said   *I cried all the way to Santa Fe*

**how many times can you pick up the downtrodden
before you say it is enough**

the words   discharged into the warmth
of a Puerto Vallarta night
for all to hear
reverberate
        uncertain if what I heard
is a question
or a statement
a conversation concluded
terminated

a table away   we are neighbours
as seaside bar-restaurants go
so   I will accept it as a question
needing a response   from the heart
after all   we are relations
in the oneness of our universe
as we watch the orange-red sun
disappear

the consequence of the words
perhaps soured by the lime margarita
you are holding in one hand
while the other is raised to the heavens
in some grand gesture
as if bull riding is burdensome

the captive audience of three
beautiful women at your table
with more jewellery
permissible than "the three-bling rule"
made in Mexico

inlaid white opal on silver
and pure gold   on their bodies
speaks of affluence and money

my heels cooled   let's think larger
together
the men serving us
start their day at the crack of dawn
just before the rooster's crow
like Franko   a server I met
in the bar-restaurant next door
to play his part   he awakens early
to make breakfast for his children
before he sends them off to school
separated from his wife
he works two jobs
here too   marriages fall apart

once the children are out the door
he rides the dusty buses to this side of town
to put in an honest day for 62 pesos
yes   62 pesos
that's roughly 4 dollars
I say   that is a hard-working man
in the evening   he grooms horses
for relaxation and extra pay

at the end of our precious day
you   after roasting your body red brown
in the heat of the sun's fire
me   after relaxing in the shade under the cabana

because I was born with a natural tan
the restaurant workers are always here   to greet us
like long-lost friends   like family
that is not an accident

second   I know you think you earned the right
but next time   maybe have the courage
to examine the privileged words
you release into the universe
maybe take their example   of quiet grace
looking beyond your inner circle
its larger share of wealth
to consider where it came from
it wasn't the moon
that's for sure

how many times?   you ask
the answer is simple my friend
as long as we have more to enjoy
than another   we have responsibility
to lift each other   again
and again
but even then   it may not be enough

this land   the splendour of the sunset
we came seeking tonight is borrowed
and borrowed   it must be returned
in whole or in kind

reconciled   that my friend is what I believe
okay   it's your turn

an awkward moment

(for my friend Catherine Odora Hoppers)

you want the land   but
it's occupied
what to do?   what to do?

here is a recipe for certain disaster
marinated
in a story of colonial violence

in a belief you are superior
ask the church to issue a *papal bull*   (now that's irony)
a *doctrine of discovery*
to legitimize your actions
to occupy and seize lands as your own
its inhabitants non-Christianized
and therefore   declared uncivilized

just to be certain though
that you've done the right thing
reconcile the logic of said discovery
offering the prior occupants
this tiny reserve of land
for the whole expanse of land before you   (like Big Bear said,
                                             between the lines, it
                                             wasn't yours to give
                                             away)

pay bargain sale prices to their relatives
damn the mixed bloods
offer them scrip   or cash for land far from home
while you transfer ownership
to landlords   and banks

declare the people need protection
in law and mounted enforcement
carefully crafting the pillars of justice
and orders to determine their Indian-ness   (beware it will come to
                                              haunt them; you too!)
restrict movement of said occupants
ban their languages
forbid their spiritual ceremonies
take their children away

believe in your righteousness
making certain the law is always on your side
on all matters
especially when it comes to property

omit   dehumanize and marginalize their experience
in the canon of your literatures
in schools throughout the land
making it mandatory for all to recite   (from an okiskinahamakew
                                          point of view that is truly sick)
now comes the penultimate pâstâhowin   transgression/sin
as if you could   exempt yourself
from the ethos of the land
its aliveness   its wildness   (it will haunt you)

oops!

as immense transgressions go
be wary of the generations to follow
implacable young hearts and minds
return to the land
you have taken

oh how my body trembles, how my mind reels

in the wake of the Paris massacre
a world mourns the senseless loss of promising lives
while we commemorate Louis Riel
hanged by the Canadian government
November 16   1885
41 years of age   the crime—
seeking a fair   peaceful and rightful place
for all marginalized people

today we remember the gentle man
son   brother   lover
husband   poet   father
of our beloved heart country
oh how my body trembles
how my mind reels
imagining a mother's sorrow
the senseless loss

a magnificent failure

(on Canada's 150th)

you see   Louis Riel's actions
as leader were never his alone
despite the tired   binary narrative
you keep telling yourself
was he hero or traitor
was he sane or insane?

in kinship   I offer a thread of the story
    his sister Sarah Riel
    after joining the Sisters of Charity
    lived in my home community of Île-à-la-Crosse
    where she is buried
    their paternal grandparents
    Jean Baptiste Riel and Margaret Boucher (Dene)
    met in Île-à-la-Crosse
    their father Jean-Louis was born there

you see   he was a member of a family
a member of a community of people
with a shared history and culture
tenets for kinship   human and non-human
cooperative and fiercely protective of their freedom
a member of an emerging society
oh Canada

it was inside these forces
he lived out his life and responsibilities
enmeshed as they were with his own dreams
aspirations for a good life—miyo-pimât'sowin
with all its joys and disappointments
much like our own lives today

to the very end of his short life
Louis Riel gave us all
the best of our humanity
by refusing to plead insanity

so   it is written

a controversy on prayer in public spaces

she arrives ready to listen
as granddaughter   daughter   sister
as mother   auntie   grandmother
hoping to understand
the value of prayer
in public spaces

the table tonight is set with love
representing diverse expressions of humanity
Catholic   Protestant
Jew   Hindu
Buddhist   Atheist
Muslim   Indigenous

one by one they approach the podium
bearing witness in word
to walk in justice   to practice *tolerance*
(surely   a slip of the tongue)
finally   to goodness   to God
and orderly conduct

listening   she finds herself in a quandary
once a Catholic   the Virgin Mary was constantly by her side
now   embracing every word spoken
of the heart's deepest desires
truths of belongingness and purpose
she is instantly Buddhist   Hindu   Jew   Muslim   Atheist and Protestant
already Indigenous

still   she wants to know
who invented justice?   done with tolerance!
she wants to know
on whose authority do we define
what is good?
what is orderly conduct?   done with patriarchy!

she wonders   was it God?
where does this good God stand
on this planet
its heavens in one big mess?
surely   goodness will prevail!

later   she imagines herself with others
in the *public square* of long ago
searching for answers of a lived life
her questions are very simple
who counts?   what counts?

L'dzimâsh

(for my childhood cousin-friend)

L'dzimâsh is a day you usually send out feelers into the cosmos. Maybe it comes from living alone or maybe it's a form of prayer—a reaching outward to make a connection to the human and non-human world on the day set aside for rest. Sure enough, your email arrives, and you are wondering, "what a philosopher would say: natural or divine order? Or no order at all?"

No context to draw on, I write back. I just awoke from a deep sleep! Who pray tell is asking such questions of enormous proportions? By natural order, do you mean nature's laws? By divine, do you mean God?

You respond. I am asking the question. I asked six people the same question this morning. Some views about "order" are huge, like expecting the sun to come up every morning, trees to be still standing when we wake up, even expecting the Co-op to be full of food. I was wondering about divine versus natural order after reading about how people are affected by trauma, and how trauma shakes their belief in whatever type of order they may have believed in. For instance, people who survive climate disasters or human disasters like the holocaust, wars or extreme domestic violence. It left me wondering about the kind of order I believe in, have faith in. Maybe, I need "philosopher" software to figure it out and a glass of red Beaujolais. Meanwhile, here in the boreal forest this weird climate change thing is happening. Rain in January is definitely not natural order. There is less snow than usual up here. The forests may be drier when you come this summer. Hope the blueberries aren't affected.

I offer a quick response. First off, human behaviour, judging from recent world events, would suggest we must be the most stupid life form on the planet and in the universe. Ants are smarter. And people who are traumatized by natural events or man-made disasters, of which there are so many these days, shaken in their belief about a so-called higher entity that doesn't play favourites, are sillier than silly. Let me think. I will write again.

Later that day I write. I lean toward science (from the Latin word *scientia* for knowledge)—natural laws that kihtêyak speak of, which includes growth and eventual breakdown of all life forms, sometimes helped along by other natural forces coalescing/conspiring to speed up the process. I read something interesting recently about "consciousness" that goes beyond the understanding of an awareness that resides within us as human beings, as a state extending to all life in the universe. Now that's something to wrap your head around. Never mind philosopher software, we need a Cree etymologist. It sounds vaguely familiar, like the story that everything has spirit/energy. Natural or divine order? I am not entirely certain. For now, I am content talking to plants—urging them along to maturity and beauty, singing with the birds, who seem to do so dutifully each morning. Maybe they know something we don't. I believe in purposefulness and vibration of positive energy. I believe in goodness. Most mornings, I awake happy to know there is some order and rhythm to dance to within our galaxy, regardless of where it may come from. For the most part, the pagan in me worships the old ones—sun, moon and stars, and yes, I too hope the blueberries are large, plump and juicy. There is nothing like the kiss on my lips of northern boreal sweetness, of blueberries in my mouth! That was a mouthful.

supermoon rising

busy bodies are on the street below
gathering   Saturday morning prayers

chickadees cling to branches of pine trees
a biting cold wind ruffling their feathers

the soothsayer sings as background noise   something about
tîpakîmowin î papâm wîpâsta yôtin ahci—an exacting truth blowing about
with wind

deep in thought I search for the sweet spot
ponder the murky waters of truth and reconciliation

hoping the unseen bed below is what it seems
safe for crossing   no unforeseen risks

but rivers by their nature are dynamic
we will surely stumble on our way to promised land

perhaps regain balance
in the reach of an extended hand of friendship

I am also ready for the fall
the mighty pull of the river bottom to engulf us

admittedly   I am skeptical   it's my nature
call it a precautionary measure

that anything will come of yet another report
its national *calls to action*

just this morning   âpihtaw'kosân was blowing the whistle
something amiss

respectful relations with Indigenous peoples
are on the   back burner   she warns

first governments want to ensure the middle-class majority
pockets will be lined with gold   pipelines a priority

the land   the waters   the air—well   it's all secondary
Saturday descending   larger than life   supermoon rising

October mist

    mist clings
    ground level as I walk this quietness
    the light dulled   made magnificent
    leaves of gold slowly making their way
    home to the earth beneath my feet
    like me some day   but for now I am
    content to know   it is as it always was

only two nights ago   gulls soaring high
sky a graceful movement of wings
flashes of silver against an opulent blue
I was so happy   a promise
of a quick visit from a brother
I don't see often enough

later   my happiness dashed
by a call in the wee hours of morning
speech slurred   he was now in the grips
of some evil that just won't let go
he said   *looks like I won't be making it*
for breakfast   sis

one can only lose so much

my body sank to sorrow
for the rest of the day
and into the falling night

    spilling over
    into this blue-gray morning light
    wrapped in mist

like Kumalo

(on re-reading *Cry, My Beloved Country* by Alan Patton, 1958,
on the eve of reconciliation in Canada)

like Kumalo   she travels at dusk
up a rocky winding road to a mountaintop
there   nestled among the trees and shrubs
she can see clearly
below her and to the far horizon

solitude and silence are enough to weather
this brokenness   this weariness   this hunger
she wrestles day and night
night and day
never ending

like Kumalo   she hopes
no one is on the path tonight   to ask questions
worried   her brother will not survive
but   it isn't just her brother
there are so many others   just like him

her mother   the good mother she is
always was   and always will be
will have prayed   in the quiet afternoon
when work was done
her mother still believes
bless her

like Kumalo   she has failed in her own agency
he as an ayamihâwînô   she as o-kiskinohamâkêw
words she knows carry a sacred responsibility
one   a devotion to a life of prayer
the other   to teach with future generations in mind

in the growing darkness
acahkosak—angel-stars
shining upon her
she waits to be swallowed
into a world she once knew
waves quietly   steadfastly
lapping rocks on the shoreline
a soft breeze rustling leaves
of poplar and birch
moonlight rippling
diamonds on the lake

here   on the mountaintop
she will wait for rain
to wash away the pain and sorrow
as rite of renewal   as forgiveness
as hope for this   her beloved heart country

in the morning   her eyes clouded like Kumalo
she will arise with the sun
slowly making her way
to the village   still   in the darkness below
light will glow   soon enough

when the moon is full

I will show you my flower

(another one for my dear Emerson)

come auntie   he says
taking my hand into his tiny one
I will show you   my flower

your flower?   I ask   *I love flowers*
what colour is your flower?
the colour of red oranges   he says
what can I say? he is four years old now

in slow   short   choppy steps
we walk across kohkom and moshôm's yard
across the road and into
a thicket of brush and bush

he points   *see!*
and there   is his flower
a wild orange-red Wood Lily
stem a whorl of leaves at the top
cupping its petals and sepals
tapered tipped leaves scattered
along its entire upper stem

hand in hand   we stand quietly

don't touch!   he commands

father and son

(for Paul and Matty)

senses awakened head to toe
she stares at a photograph
on a miniature elegant golden easel
a little boy
shirtless   is sitting on a log
a hot day she imagines

a paint brush in hand
his concentration is on an image
he is painting on one of two sheets of paper
placed on the lap of a young man
sitting close beside him
staring out into valley and beyond

both seem oblivious
to what the other is doing
each intent on capturing
what lies in front of them
a valley of green abundance
a field of golden grasses
bursts of yellow and orange leaves

when she enters the frame
she remembers
she was the one
behind the eye of the camera
wanting to hold on .
to the image in front of her

she notes it was an autumn day
when unbeknownst to the painters
a bond of trust and friendship
took shape and form in broad brush strokes
their oneness woven
in flesh   in blood   in spirit
on a hillside along a valley

at Spadina and 21st

leaning against the lamppost
like it might save him from a fall
she remembers him saying (unequivocally)
I cannot live without you.
has anyone ever told you
there is no match for your beauty
here in Saskatoon   Saskatchewan
in Canada
or the whole wide world for that matter?

such charm   she blushed
all the way to *sa-ki-ta-wak   Île-à-la-Crosse*
a skinny girl behind a telephone pole
who loved to hide from people all day
and then back to the sidewalk
in front of the famous castle hotel
at Spadina and 21st

in response to his kindness
she remembers her words (elongated)
Sas ka toooon   Sas katch eeee wan
such a beautiful place name
don't you think?
it's Cree you know!

what's your name   again?

those deadly beasts

bring a zapinator   there are wasps
living under your steps   my cousin warns

wasps!   oh no! those deadly beasts! I think
my attitude larger than a little winged creature
that has such impeccable taste
for moose bourguignon   wild rice and red wine

head down in shame   I ask myself
what's in the attitude bush baby?
surely   they are godly creatures
in a revolutionary way of thinking
they were put on this earth
to do something   they have purpose

trusting my instinct   I begin my voyage
into the global darkness of the web
unearthing   excavating
every piece of information
I can dig up

wasps primarily feed on insects
pests that devour our crops
insects that spread disease
tapwe ici—is this the truth?
someone should have told me this story long ago
they sting and can annoy us
but they are key to keeping down
other pesky insects and pests
that do damage to our well-being

like us   they are looking for protein
sugar   your wine   to survive
so   next time show them some r e s p e c t
like you often do   to those loveable bumble bees
that pollinate plants
so   we can survive and multiply

wasps are valuable
economic, social and environmental   holy!
before long   I have changed my tune
the can of poison I armed myself with
from the Big River Co-op
will remain untouched

that is . . . until the next wasp flies
into and under my yellow flowered skirt
zings me one big fat   blue bruise

daylight thief at Amigos Café

a gentle man with broad
generous shoulders   slightly overweight
leans forward   laughter in his belly
captured in the orbit of an attractive woman
I watch her   reach slowly across the table
to caress his hand

at another table   a young man sits
across from an older woman   possibly his mother
they are deep in conversation
as he wrings his hands over and over
I watch her
gently take both his hands into hers

at another table   sit four adults chatting
while a little girl dances   dosey does
hanging onto the back of a chair   and then another
the grown-ups oblivious   to her joy
I watch   take her into my gaze
she smiles   nods   resumes her dance

heart full   I ponder
the cold   stringy carrot coconut soup
in front of me   aware
I have been sitting alone staring out into the world
a thief   in broad daylight
stealing the sacred   all around me

the weather channel

on most days   she rises early
to watch the weather channel
today is fair but cooling   says the weatherman
as he maps the course of her unfolding life

even double digits can't take the chill out
socks and sweaters in the middle of May
it wasn't always this way   double digits
were a sure sign of spring-come-summer

Wednesday is calling for scattered showers
swept   she weeps for her own life
the could-have-beens and should-have-beens
so unlike her to live with regret

cooler still on Thursday   says the weatherman
with clouds breaking during the day
it is her heart breaking
she was born in winter   konita awasis   child in vain

but loved and cherished she was   · nonetheless
today   she understood that soon
she would cease to live
reluctantly   against her will

forecast for Friday is sunny and warm
it's what she has been waiting to hear all morning
come Friday night   she will be stepping out
into starlight   to dance the night away

night thief on 11ᵗʰ street

she awakens to delicate clinking sounds of glass
her ears like wapiti trying to pinpoint the source

in darkness   she reaches for the bedside clock
it is 2 a.m.   listens for the sound again

finding her glasses on the bedside table
she peers out of the bedroom window

under bluish neon light   she catches
a small figure of a human form

rummaging through the blue recycle bin
she placed on the curb late   last night

she stands by the window   as still as can be
watching as they comb through her recyclables

placing chosen items carefully
into a container on the ground

when they pick up their belongings   signaling a move
down the street   she wants to follow

to stay in this moment of grace
in the simple   elegance of this night

words and beads, lines and silk threads

you know you are Métis when
you salivate
hearing certain sounds
lapocin   l'frrakasî
li rrababô   mîn'sâpoy
la kalet   l' boyöň

you know you are Métis when
you confuse "vingt" with "l'vǎň"
your grandfather is counting weights
on the net   he has been mending all morning
you run to tell your grandmother
certain   moshôm has drinking on his mind

you know you are Métis when
you weep instead of dance
at the sound of the fiddle
remembering your uncle Louis
late evenings on the porch
playing melancholic music to the universe

you know you are Métis when
your auntie Pauline claims
at a family wake
that *Breeze* has nothing over the heavenly scent
of wet   stiff   frozen underwear
hung on the clothesline in winter
then wrestled into the house to dry

you know you are Métis when
your eyes hurt so bad
at the sight of a handsome man
who swaggers into a room
poignantly stops   combs his dark hair back
with his fingers in a stroke of a strong hand

you know you are Métis when
you realize you are related to everyone
based on the family tree
passed down to you as a young woman
and there is no one   I mean no one
for miles around available to marry

you know you are Métis when
you believe   squirrels are relatives
you believe   when it rains
they are crying   replenishing the earth
revelation an on-going process
    we really do not know much

you know you are Métis when
you greet everyone you meet with
oh Milky Way galax-yion!   oh earthling!
how spectacular our home!
did you know   from the vantage point of lalôn
    we disappear

you know you are Métis when
you talk about wild life
you don't mean
trees and plants or animals in the boreal forest
fowl or birds or rodents   you mean
the life you actually lead or wish you did

you know you are Métis when
you are wearing designer jeweller   *Pelletier*
gems of real stones
intricately tangled in seed beads
and you want the world
to know   you are

when the moon is full

she fills the night sky
calling out   *look at me! look at me!*

not tonight   please   I plead
fragile from nightly news
afraid to look at her luminous fullness
the world gone mad
only comfort is knowing
I am not alone
in this waking
nightmare

the mass killings
of innocent men and women
children and babies   unborn
the logics of men
with guns and bullets   planes and missiles
mâmaskâc—incredulous!

the weight of colonial history
no escape from the ugliness of bigotry
the ravages of greed   poverty

a desire to know what makes us human
as if knowing might save me—
and when I say me
I mean us

tonight   bathing in the blueness of her light
I succumb to her terrestrial tide
as I journey home once again to the land
of muskeg   birch   poplar   spruce   sandy beaches

you are some beauty   some beauty! I call out
and then   she follows me all the way
into the safety of my tiny blue house
filled with memories   miyo sâkihitowin—a sacred love

a new day is here

she awoke   a mantra in her head
wan'skâ   n'dzânis! wan'skâ!   wake up
birds have finished their morning songs
and kohkoms their morning invocations

in the news this morning
an eagle was released   after being nurtured
by the caring hands of a young man

he and his workmates had found the eagle
dying from toxic poisoning

the young man said of the eagle:
he just flat out couldn't eat
or speak

he couldn't use his legs
couldn't even stand up   and
he was vomiting quite a lot

but   the eagle was a feisty one
fighting back in the throes of delirium
finally submitting to his captors

today   he was released
he took wing   soaring
high into the sky

he then returned to his captors
in graceful flight   swooping
circling above them five   six times

crying out
marrsî   my relatives!   marrsî!
you have been most kind!

the rest of us will carry you along

in the quiet of an afternoon in isolation

a pungent scent of soap
overwhelms my senses
as I walk into the laundry
where my auntie Albertine works

against the north wall
a row of giant washing machines
are whirring soap suds
through the looking glass
of each gyrating machine

on a large oblong table
are baskets full of white
freshly washed linens and clothing
ready to be hung on the clothesline
lining the perimeter
of the mission hospital grounds
and piles of dry laundry
ready for ironing and folding

it is a wash day
at the laundry
where she has worked
since I can remember

my auntie is standing
in the middle of the room
facing the grand circular drum
of a gigantic iron
sweat pouring off her face

she greets me with a smile
words unnecessary
joins me in one corner
of her work area
hands me a white gown to wear

as she completes the ironing
of sheets and pillowcases
she hands them to me
to fold as she has taught me
end to end with tight folds

my auntie is one of the best
seamstresses I know
she is also one of the best
upholsterers I know
before I could even say the word
in this small village
without many amenities

the corner of the laundry room
reserved for sewing and upholstery
is her favorite place to be
when the laundry is done

auntie is my mother's younger sister
she is like a mother to me

ode to Albertine

the ring you gave me
on your death bed
to size
when you were gone
later a change of heart
it was just for safe keeping
I shouldn't size it   yet
in case you had more time
    has never been sized

whenever I think I might have lost
that ring   its tiniest of diamonds
a person can miss   not looking closely enough
I lose my head
not sure   if I will live
another day without it

its sparkle is you across the room
eyes twinkling   back at me
a memory of a hopeful moment
you might pull through
from the cancer ravaging your body

holding your hand in mine
to your last breath
I never wanted to let you go
it was your sister   my birth mother
who convinced me   it was time
to set your spirit free

every now and again
you appear in my dreams
yesterday   we were visiting and laughing
across the table of your sunflower-filled kitchen
you were showing off
your latest garage-sale treasures

when I shared the story
of your recent visitation with my mother
I became grief struck   I couldn't speak
knowingly   she nodded her head
walked over and sat beside me
rocking back and forth
in silence
     until I could speak again

a table in the sky

On a warm summer day, I will come to you to say let's go down the Beaver River to visit family, and you will oblige my fancy like you always do. I will promise to take responsibility to prepare the grub box, filling it with food to take with us for sustenance when we break for lunch and a rest. I have much to make up for. It is my turn to give.

I will have prepared fresh lakalet made with butter for this special day. I will have prepared your favourite—l'pwasöň l'boyöň, lî patak êkwa lî korrot ahci. Lî cizayöň mîna for garnish from my special plot in the garden you set aside just for me in front of our house. Instead of the boughs of some sweet sapling for our table, I will sneak out with two of grandma's beautifully embroidered linen dishtowels when she isn't looking, to spread on the ground when it is time to eat. I will beg her forgiveness upon return. To quench your thirst, I will have filled your thermos with tea and a touch of sugar, just the way you like it.

I am looking forward to meandering our way down the reed-clustered river, the sounds of duck quacks all about, an occasional crow cawing us from the shoreline, the river breeze on our skin and a warm sun on our faces. From time to time, I will look back to watch you steer the boat to make sure you are still with me in body, knowing your spirit will be soaring on some far-off journey. Even then you will hold that heightened sense of consciousness I could never understand as a little girl. I think I do now. You will smile at me as if to say how happy you are to be together on this journey down the river, once again. I will smile back as if to say, marrsî pâpâ for all you have given me—a way of being with others in silence, a way of saying I love you without a word, a way of seeing through difficult and good times—simply in a presence that only love knows.

the rest of us will carry you along

still reeling from apocalyptic images
humans in sterile white full-body suits
tanks of a disinfectant agent on their backs
spacewalk   fumigating deserted streets of Wuhan

the city morgues of New York
filling to capacity   along with hospitals
their corridors lined with COVID-19 patients
struggling for breath and for their lives

gross statistics and morbidity analysis
of the sick and dying are rolling in
there is nothing new to this story
its failures or shortcomings

we were never in this together
all risks written down
in reports collecting dust somewhere
mapping lives of marginalized   easily forgotten people

a willful blindness to history and to suffering
old ones isolated in nursing homes   or drafty apartments
lives of loved ones at risk   compromised
by poverty   a lottery called life

I am growing tired of all the noise
trying to snare me
frantic with busyness
numbness so I forget

all the people without clean water
to drink or wash their hands
no nutritious food to put on the table to stay healthy
people without meaningful work

just meagre wages without benefits
at the mercy of vulture corporations
generating profits for a handful of billionaires
asking governments for tax exemptions

bailouts   but don't call it *welfare* oh no!
I sit in silence staring out into nothingness
when a heavenly-sent message lands on my desk—
a summons to mindful meditation from a poet friend

call it prayer if you want   quells my anger
all I want to do now is grieve
bearing witness to the cruelty of *thinking*
some lives are expendable

for a moment   I catch my breath
breathing along in spirit
with others across the land
for those who have a hard time breathing

for a moment in time
we are   *a communal respirator for the sick*
breathing in and out   in and out
in and out   gently now   gently

sorrowful sky

I reach out into the mysterious depth of the unknown
now on this nth day of self-isolation   grieving

a strong gust of spring wind promises to lift my spirit
in the measure of clouds swirling across a fearless blue sky

white-headed gulls soar high overhead
a choreography of wings   each the span of a butterfly's wing

from this vantage point   I touch sky   holding her white ribbons
of cloud in my hands   an invocation for the sick and the dying

Notes

1. "like children" contains a collage of excerpted lines from three of the late Greg Younging's poems in *The Random Flow of Blood and Flowers* (Ekstasis Editions, 1996).

2. *"oh how my body trembles, how my mind reels"* is a line borrowed from "How My Body Trembles," a poem written by Louis Riel as he awaited his execution. Savoie, P. (translation), Campbell, G. (editor), *Selected Poetry of Louis Riel* (Exile Editions, 2000), 125.

3. *"a magnificent failure"* is borrowed from an observation made by Guy Lavallee (1992) in his homily delivered at a mass in Winnipeg at a Métis Cultural Reunion. He stated, "Perhaps, Louis Riel failed to solve the problems of the Métis people of his time, but the Métis consider it a magnificent failure, which only increases his greatness. Riel's ideals were and are worthy yet today, his actions were honourable and his devotion was for the people."

4. *"the rest of us will carry you along"* is inspired by Sue Goyette and a story attending a live performance by Jeremy Dutcher. On this occasion he invited his audience to sing along with him. Jeremy told his audience before they started to carry on even if they lost their breath momentarily, telling them, *the rest of us will carry you along.*

5. The following poems have appeared in journals, in print and online: "a new day is here" and "he hasn't entirely lost his touch" appeared in *ndn country*, a joint issue of *CV2* and *Prairie Fire* in 2018; "a beautiful rebellion" and "deeper than bone" appeared in a special issue of *Grain Magazine* in 2019; "October mist" and "like Kumalo" appear in the University of Saskatchewan's online MFA Variety Show; "blood on the snow" and "supermoon rising" appeared in *Grain Magazine* in fall 2021; and "holy, holy, holy" and "ode to jackpine" appeared in *Event Magazine*, in fall 2021. "deeper than bone" was selected for *Best Canadian Poetry 2020* by Biblioasis.

ninanâskomon—I am thankful

As I write these words of thankfulness, Environment Canada has issued a heat warning for communities in Saskatchewan's northern boreal forest, and so I am thankful for the cool breeze coming off the lake this morning. Soon, I will have to shut all the windows and hope the tall spruce trees standing in front of my tiny blue house, planted by the missionaries, will provide sufficient shade for the remainder of the day. Last night, I heard from my cousins that many of the old spruce trees planted along the shoreline and grotto in our community were being cut down. I was filled with a momentary sadness. I will miss them and perhaps the shoreline will too. But I digress. I am thankful that Thistledown Press is willing to take a chance on my poetry, once again. I am thankful for Randy Lundy's willingness to lend his poetic intelligence and sensibility to my draft manuscript. *We* hope *we* made the right decision when *we* decided to remove just about all of the periods for consistency and aesthetic reasons. I am thankful for the friendship and support I have received over the years from Vince Ahenakew, a fluent speaker and writer of northern Michif. I am thankful for the professional comradery of Viz Ink—their love of words and telling of a story. I couldn't ask for a better circle of writer friends. And yes, I am thankful for my favourite critic, Paul Jacoby. Once an English teacher, always an English teacher. I am thankful for the financial support and recognition of my work by The Hnatyshyn Foundation through their 2017 *REVEAL — Indigenous Arts Awards*. Finally, I am thankful to the Saskatchewan Writers Guild for the sense of community they create through their overall programming, including the recognition provided through the *John V. Hicks Long Manuscript Awards*, in which I placed second for this manuscript in 2021. marrsî kahkiyaw awiyak—thank you to everyone!

RITA BOUVIER is a Métis writer and educator from Saskatchewan. Her third book of poetry, *nakamowin'sa* for the seasons (Thistledown Press, 2015), was the 2016 Saskatchewan Book Awards winner of the Rasmussen, Rasmussen & Charowsky Aboriginal Peoples' Writing Award. Rita's poetry has appeared in literary anthologies, journals—print and online—musicals, and television productions, and has been translated into Spanish, German and the Cree-Michif of her home community of sakitawak, Île-à-la-Crosse, situated on the historic trading and meeting grounds of Cree and Dene people.